THE HIGGS MECHANISM
EXPLAINED

THE MYSTERIES OF SPACE

THE HIGGS MECHANISM EXPLAINED

JARYD ULBRICHT

Enslow Publishing
101 W. 23rd Street
Suite 240
New York, NY 10011
USA

enslow.com

Published in 2019 by Enslow Publishing, LLC.
101 W. 23rd Street, Suite 240, New York, NY 10011

Copyright © 2019 by Enslow Publishing, LLC.
All rights reserved.

No part of this book may be reproduced by any means without the written permission of the publisher.

Library of Congress Cataloging-in-Publication Data

Names: Ulbricht, Jaryd, author.
Title: The Higgs mechanism explained / Jaryd Ulbricht.
Description: New York : Enslow Publishing, [2019] | Series: The mysteries of space | Audience: Grades 7 to 12. | Includes bibliographical references and index.
Identifiers: LCCN 2017057609| ISBN 9780766099593 (library bound) | ISBN 9780766099609 (pbk.)
Subjects: LCSH: Higgs bosons—Juvenile literature. | Particles (Nuclear physics)—Juvenile literature. | Field theory (Physics)—Juvenile literature. | Grand unified theories (Nuclear physics)—Juvenile literature.
Classification: LCC QC793.5.B62 U43 2018 | DDC 539.7/21—dc23
LC record available at https://lccn.loc.gov/2017057609

Printed in the United States of America

To Our Readers: We have done our best to make sure all website addresses in this book were active and appropriate when we went to press. However, the author and the publisher have no control over and assume no liability for the material available on those websites or on any websites they may link to. Any comments or suggestions can be sent by email to customerservice@enslow.com.

Photos Credits: Cover Pasieka/Science Photo Library/Getty Images; p. 7 Owls Photography/Shutterstock.com; p. 11 Hulton Archive/Getty Images; p. 13 snapgalleria/Shutterstock.com; pp. 14, 15 Fouad A. Saad/Shutterstock.com; p. 18 Mopic/Shutterstock.com; p. 21 XiXinXing/Shutterstock.com; p. 23 Pictorial Parade/Archive Photos/Getty Images; pp. 24, 51, 52 adapted from diagrams provided by the author; p. 27 Peter Hermes Furian/Shutterstock.com; pp. 29, 34 udaix/Shutterstock.com; p. 31 Dorling Kindersley/Getty Images; p. 33 photoiconix/Shutterstock.com; pp. 40, 44, 49, 57, 64, 65, 67 Designua/Shutterstock.com; p. 54 Miguel Riopa/AFP/Getty Images; p. 60 Lionel Flusin/Gamma-Rapho/Getty Images; p. 66 RIA Novosti/Science Source; back cover and interior pages sdecoret/Shutterstock.com (earth's atmosphere from space), clearviewstock/Shutterstock.com (space and stars).

CONTENTS

Introduction
6

Chapter One
Making Sense of Mass
9

Chapter Two
Symmetries in Physics
20

Chapter Three
Particles and Waves
26

Chapter Four
The Standard Model
38

Chapter Five
The Higgs Mechanism
48

Chapter Six
Beyond the Standard Model
62

Chapter Notes 69
Glossary 74
Further Reading 77
Index 79

INTRODUCTION

Why is it harder to throw a bowling ball than a baseball? Intuitively this question seems to have a simple answer: the bowling ball is larger, it is made of more stuff. But why is it harder to throw something that is made of more stuff than something that is made of less stuff? One might also try to ask this question quantitatively: is throwing two baseballs taped together twice as hard? Or is it one and a half times as hard? Or three times as hard?

Physics attempts to explain the universe in concrete terms. If something is described as large, what does that mean exactly? An apple is large compared to an ant, but an apple is small in comparison to a house. For this reason, physics is written in the language of mathematics. Stated in the language of mathematics, a bowling ball is thirty-four to thirty-five times harder to throw than a baseball.

Stating how much harder it is to throw a bowling ball than a baseball doesn't answer the original question though: why is it harder? To describe how the motion of an object changes, the concept of force is introduced. A force is a measure of how hard one pushes or pulls on an object. An example of a force is weight, which is the force Earth's gravity applies on nearby objects. Typically force is measured in Newtons (N), but it is

INTRODUCTION

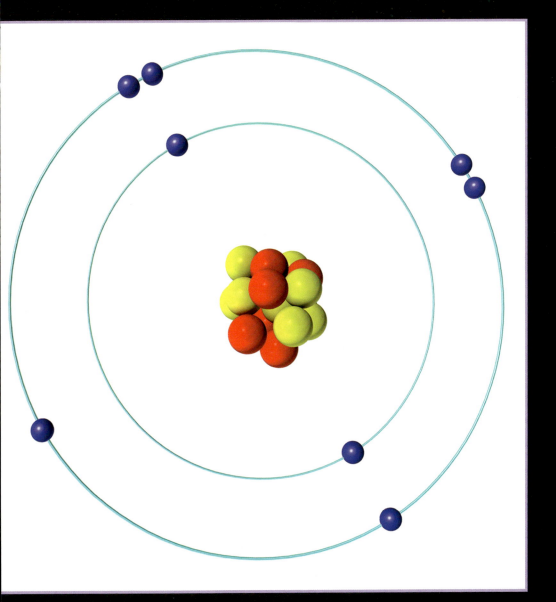

All matter is composed of atoms, which are further broken down into protons (*red*), neutrons (*yellow*), and electrons (*blue*).

7

also commonly measured in pounds (lbs). Your weight can be converted from pounds to Newtons by multiplying your weight in pounds by 4.45. For example, the average weight of an adult female in the United States is 166.2 pounds. That multiplied by 4.45 is 739.59 Newtons. Weight is often described in kilograms (kg), but this is actually a mass, not a weight. One kilogram on the surface of Earth *weighs* 9.8 Newtons (2.02 lbs), but it is not *equal to* 9.8 Newtons (2.02 lbs).

A heavy car weighs more than a bicycle because Earth exerts a larger force on the car than it does on the bicycle. Similarly, it requires more force to accelerate a bowling ball than a baseball. The reason is because a bowling ball has more mass than a baseball. And the force required to accelerate an object is proportional to its mass.

So what is this thing called mass? In order to answer this very fundamental question, one has to talk about the basic building blocks of matter. Baseballs and bowling balls are composed of molecules, which are made of atoms, which in turn are comprised of electrons, protons, and neutrons. The most basic objects that scientists know of are called elementary particles, and they are grouped together in a physical theory known as the standard model.

There's a problem though: in the standard model, none of the particles can have mass because that would violate a basic symmetry principle. But looking around, one can see things do have mass. How can the standard model be a theory of the universe on the smallest scales but not have masses? The answer is due to a very special subatomic particle in the standard model: the Higgs boson.

Chapter One

Making Sense of Mass

The Higgs mechanism is a procedure that makes massless particles massive. But what is mass? How does one tell if something is massive? Analogously, anyone who has ever been swimming in the ocean has probably noticed that the water has an unusual flavor. Ocean water contains a lot of sodium chloride (NaCl), or salt. When ocean water gets in someone's mouth, they are tasting the salt, so they says it tastes salty. But what does salt taste like? Saying salt tastes "salty" doesn't tell us anything. It's just a circular statement: of course it tastes like salt—it is salt! This is the same problem with defining mass. In the same way, mass is a property of a massive object.

Measuring Mass

Defining mass is not straightforward, but people actually have a relatively easy time recognizing something that has mass and that more massive objects are harder to move. It's easy to test whether something is massive or not: try to change the object's motion (slow it down or speed it up). If the object resists that change in motion, it has mass. A change in motion is called an acceleration. Objects that don't have a lot of mass will still provide some resistance, but it might be harder to feel because it is so small.

Another way to tell if something is massive is to weigh it on a scale. However, one needs to be very careful when comparing weight and mass. Weight is a force. An object's weight can change just by moving it, from Earth to Mars for instance, because the gravity is weaker on Mars than it is on Earth, but its mass will remain the same. An object's weight depends on its gravitational mass, but talking about how hard it is to push something refers to its inertial mass. Yes, there is more than one kind of mass. In fact, there are at least seven different kinds of mass![1]

The three kinds of mass most important to this discussion of the Higgs mechanism are inertial mass (a measure of an object's resistance to acceleration), active gravitational mass (a measure of how much gravity an object creates), and passive gravitational mass (a measure of how much an object reacts to being in a gravitational field). So what is the difference between these masses? Conceptually there is no reason to believe that inertial mass and gravitational mass should be related at all. However, extremely precise measurements cannot tell them apart, which is an important fact.

Weak Equivalence Principle

Galileo Galilei was the first to show the equivalence of gravitational mass and inertial mass. Born in Pisa, Italy, in 1564, Galileo changed the course of humanity by developing the

MAKING SENSE OF MASS

The story goes that Galileo dropped objects of varying mass from the top of the Tower of Pisa to demonstrate how the acceleration of an object in free fall is independent of the object's mass. This experiment may have never happened, but the conclusion is correct.

scientific method. By combining experiment with mathematics, he showed the motion of objects to be mathematical in nature. Galileo found that the acceleration of an object in free fall (the motion of objects under the influence of gravity and no other forces) is independent of its mass.[2] This could only be true if the object's passive gravitational mass was exactly equal to its inertial mass; this became known as the weak equivalence principle. Astronaut David Scott observed the same result during the 1971 *Apollo 15* mission, when he dropped a hammer and a feather simultaneously from shoulder height on the moon. In the absence of an atmosphere to slow the feather down, the hammer and the feather hit the ground at the same time, even though the hammer was much more massive than the feather.[3]

Following in the footsteps of Galileo, Sir Isaac Newton (1643–1727) took the physics world by storm. Newton was perhaps the greatest mind ever to walk the earth, having formulated the laws of motion and universal gravitation by the time he was just twenty-five. He developed the mathematics of calculus independently alongside Gottfried Wilhelm Leibniz (1646–1716) and used it to frame his theories on the motion of the planets. Newton refined Galileo's work on mass with his three laws:

1. Inertia: An object either remains at rest or continues to move at a constant velocity, unless acted upon by a force.
2. $\vec{F} = m\vec{a}$: The sum of the forces $\vec{F}$ acting on a object is equal to the mass of the object m multiplied by the acceleration $\vec{a}$ of the object.
3. Equal and opposite reactions: When one body exerts a force on a second body, the second body simultaneously exerts a force equal in magnitude and opposite in direction on the first body.

Newton's first law states that an object with inertial mass will continue to move with the same velocity unless one tries to change its motion. This illustrates how inertial mass is defined: instead of explaining what it is, one defines objects with inertial mass by how they behave. Newton's second law shows how to calculate mass: exert a force on an object and measure its acceleration, plug those numbers into $F = ma \rightarrow m = \frac{F}{a}$, and determine the mass. Now that mass can be calculated, it is time

MAKING SENSE OF MASS

Thrust

A rocket is propelled upward by accelerating expanding gas in the opposite direction of the rocket's motion. When the rocket runs out of fuel it will no longer provide an upward thrust, and if the rocket is in deep space, it will continue to move with a constant velocity after all the fuel is spent. If the rocket is near Earth's surface when it runs out of fuel, gravity will act as an external force on the rocket, causing it to accelerate downward.

THE HIGGS MECHANISM EXPLAINED

to introduce some more units. Time is measured in seconds (s). Distance is measured in meters (m). An object's velocity is the change in the object's position per change in time, so velocity has units of $\frac{meters}{seconds}$ or $\frac{m}{s}$. An acceleration is a change in an object's velocity per change in time, so it has units of $\frac{m}{s^2}$. If a $5N$ force is

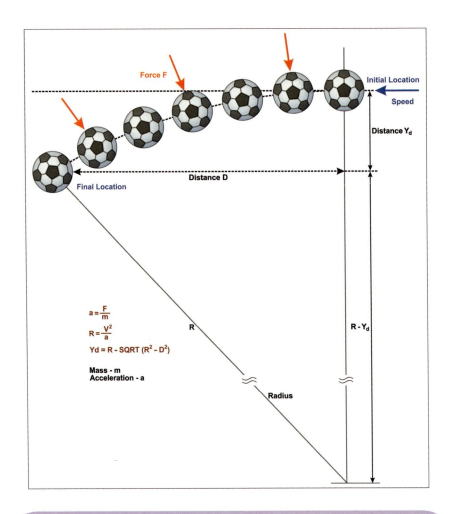

In a demonstration of Newton's second law, a soccer ball accelerates toward the center of a circular path due to the presence of a net external force.

MAKING SENSE OF MASS

applied on an object and one measures its acceleration to be $2\frac{m}{s^2}$ then the object has a mass of

$$m = \frac{F}{a} = \frac{5N}{2\frac{m}{s^2}} = 2.5 kg$$

where kilograms (kg) is the measure of an object's inertial mass. Newton's third law states that there are no isolated forces, meaning that forces always come in pairs. The use of the word "simultaneous" means that even though it is said that *one*

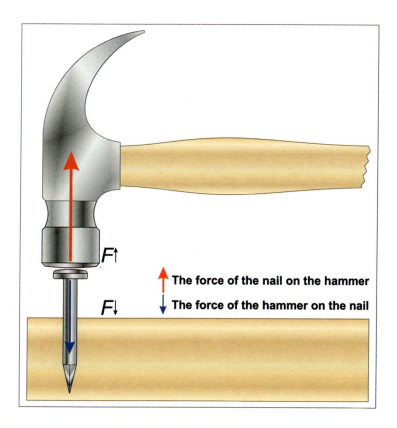

The force of the nail on the hammer
The force of the hammer on the nail

The hammer exerts a downward force on the nail, driving it into the wooden plank. Simultaneously the nail exerts an upward force on the hammer, causing the hammer to decelerate and eventually come to a stop after the collision..

THE HIGGS MECHANISM EXPLAINED

object exerts a force on a second object and the *second object* reacts with an equal and opposite force, there is no distinction between the object being acted on and the object doing the acting. If a hammer applies a force on a nail by hitting it, it is the same as a hammer being hit by a nail with that same force

DEFINING A MEASURE OF MASS

In 1795, the gram, one-thousandth of a kilogram, was defined as the mass of one cubic centimeter of water at the melting point of ice. One gram is rather small though, so the kilogram was adopted as the International System of Units (SI) base unit of mass. The International Prototype of the Kilogram (IPK, or *Le Grande K*) is a cylinder made of 90 percent platinum and 10 percent iridium stored by the International Bureau of Weights and Measures in Saint-Cloud, France, that has a mass of exactly one kilogram. Since 1889, the IPK has defined the kilogram so that all other measurements of mass are really just relations to the mass of the IPK. Several copies of the IPK have been manufactured and distributed across the world so that other nations can compare masses, but it has recently been observed that the mass of the IPK has been decreasing relative to the masses of its copies. What is causing the change in mass is still unknown, but it has far-reaching implications. Many other units of measure are defined based off of the kilogram, so if the definition of the kilogram changes, so do all the units based off of it.

in the opposite direction. Newton also came up with the law of universal gravitation, which states that all objects with mass exert a gravitational force on other objects with mass.

Strong Equivalence Principle

Another example of Newton's third law is illustrated by riding in an elevator: the person's weight is a downward force causing the elevator to accelerate toward the ground, and the elevator applies an upward force on the person, keeping them from simply falling down the elevator shaft. But what if the cable supporting the elevator snaps, and the rider and the elevator fall freely under the influence of gravity? What would the rider experience? The elevator rider would feel weightless, as if they were floating in the vacuum of empty space. Now imagine this person were actually in space, inside a spaceship shaped like an elevator with rockets attached to the floor. As the rockets ignited and accelerated the elevator-ship toward Alpha Centauri (the closest star system to Earth), the floor of the elevator would apply a force on them, and they would apply an equal and opposite force on the elevator floor. The effect would feel like standing in an elevator right here on Earth! So if they were in an elevator and couldn't look outside through a window, could they tell the difference between being in space and being on Earth? If they found themselves floating, they could either be moving at a constant velocity in space or the elevator cable has broken. If the elevator floor is applying a force on them (and them on the elevator floor), they are either standing in an elevator that isn't moving on Earth or they are in a spaceship accelerating toward some nearby star. The equivalence between these two

THE HIGGS MECHANISM EXPLAINED

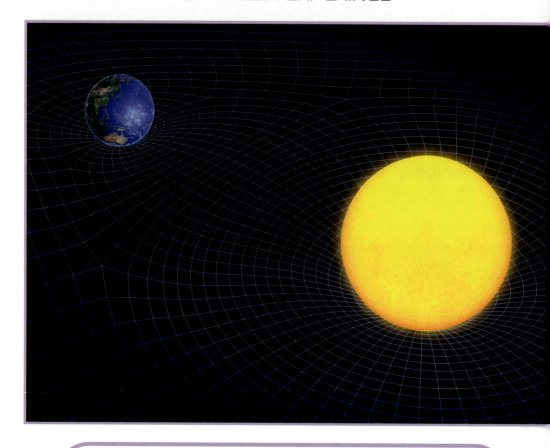

The mass (and energy) from Earth and the sun causes space and time to curve. Earth follows the curvature of space, tracing out an elliptical path around the sun.

situations stimulated the mind of another famous physicist: Albert Einstein.

Einstein (1879–1955) was confounded by this issue with elevators, acceleration, and gravity. He formulated a solution to the problem, which he published in 1916 and called general relativity.[4] General relativity asserts that anything with energy causes space and time to stretch and bend, and the bending and stretching is felt as gravity. There is much to be said about general relativity, but the most important thing to this discussion of mass is as follows: the energy of a particle E at rest is its inertial mass m times the speed of light (c) squared ($E = mc^2$). Because energy causes space-time to curve, and mass is just a form of energy, mass causes space-time to curve. Going further, because the curvature of space-time is what we feel as gravity, mass creates gravity! This became what is now known as the strong equivalence principle.

Chapter Two

Symmetries in Physics

A symmetry is a property of an object or system such that a change to that object or system leaves it indistinguishable from itself before the change was made. As an example, consider a person's image in a mirror versus a photograph. How would one tell which image is the photograph and which is the reflection? If there was writing on the person's shirt one could distinguish the two images because the letters would be reversed in the reflection, but for the most part, people are left/right symmetric. Most animals are also left/right symmetric. If you woke up tomorrow and the entire world switched right with left how long would it take for you to realize something had changed?

The idea of symmetries is very important to physics. A lot can be learned about the universe by changing something and observing what stays the same. Symmetries go far beyond reflections of images and can include transformations such as reversing the direction of time or changing the sign of the electric

A reflection is an example of a symmetry. Performing complicated tasks while looking at a mirror is often difficult because a direction is reflected. It takes practice to learn how to compensate for this reflection and accomplish such dexterous feats as tying a neck tie.

THE HIGGS MECHANISM EXPLAINED

charge of a particle. Symmetries can be broken up into two main categories: discrete and continuous. A continuous symmetry can be broken up into ever smaller pieces and performed gradually. A discrete symmetry must be performed all at once. An example of a continuous symmetry is the rotation of a ball. A ball can be rotated by 5° or 10° or 107.4°, and it will look exactly the same. In fact, a ball can be continuously rotated by any amount and it will always appear just as it did before being rotated, assuming that the ball has no writing or distinguishing marks on it. An example of a discrete symmetry is a reflection. A reflection turns one or more

MIRROR IMAGE

One normally thinks of mirrors as reversing left and right, but that isn't quite correct. A mirror reverses the forward/backward directions, so that if you are facing north, your mirror image faces south. East and west for your mirror image are still east and west for you, likewise with up and down. To prove this, turn your head sideways and look into a mirror with your right ear facing up; it should now appear as if your mirror self's right ear is facing down. How does the mirror know to flip left with right when you are standing upright, and to switch up with down when you are facing sideways? It doesn't because the mirror isn't switching up with down or right with left; it's reversing the forward/backward directions.

directions into the opposite directions (e.g., right → left, and left → right), but a reflection can never be performed halfway—it's all or nothing. Both types of symmetries are important to physics, but it was continuous symmetries that were the subject of a theorem proposed by German mathematician Emmy Noether (1882–1935) that allowed physicists of the early twentieth century to formulate consistent theories of quantum mechanics.

Emmy Noether, pictured here c. 1930, made groundbreaking discoveries in both mathematics and science and is widely believed to have been one of the most influential persons in theoretical physics.

THE HIGGS MECHANISM EXPLAINED

Emmy Noether pioneered the fields of abstract algebra and theoretical physics. In 1915, Noether wrote her seminal paper on symmetries and conservation laws in physics. It became known as Noether's theorem and has been called "one of the most important mathematical theorems ever proved in guiding the development of modern physics."[1] What Noether found was that continuous symmetries imply conservation laws. The things

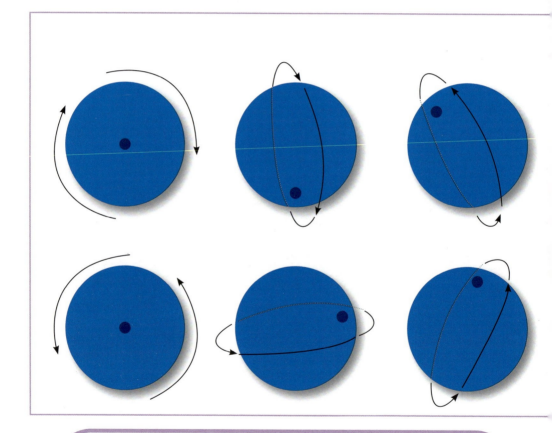

An unblemished ball can be rotated about its center without appearing to change in any way. However, adding a mark breaks the ball's symmetry, allowing one to differentiate between the various directions in which the ball is rotating.

that are conserved are typically called charges but also include energy and momentum. For instance, the spherical symmetry of a ball implies that if it is rotating it will continue to rotate at the same rate, and if it is not rotating it will not suddenly start to rotate. In the case of the ball, the thing that is conserved is the angular momentum, essentially the rate of rotation of the ball.

At the core of the Higgs mechanism is a symmetry called a special unitary transformation. Special unitary transformations are almost the same as rotating a ball. A ball is spherically symmetric, but if someone marks a point on the surface of the ball with a dot, different orientations of the ball will be easily distinguishable. The ball still has one rotational symmetry: rotations that leave the dot in the same location. Placing the dot on the ball therefore reduces the number of rotations that leave the ball indistinguishable. The Higgs mechanism works the same way: there are four Higgs bosons that can be rotated around (like the unblemished ball). The symmetry is eventually broken (like placing a dot on the ball), leaving only one physical Higgs boson, while the other three get absorbed into other particles, giving the other particles mass.

Chapter Three

Particles and Waves

Humans have often wondered "Of what is something made?" Can matter be broken down to an infinite degree? Or is there some minimum scale at which matter is no longer divisible? Empedocles (c. 490–430 BCE) theorized that everything is made of just four elements: earth, water, air, and fire.[1] The motion of objects is determined by composition and their wanting to be together: fire-like objects rise to the heavens, whereas earth-like things fall to the ground. Democritus (c. 460–c. 370 BCE) was one of the earliest proponents of atomism, in which all things are composed of small geometric shapes. These tiny "atoms" were fundamental, meaning they could not be decomposed into smaller components.[2]

Particles of Matter

René Descartes (1596–1650) put forth a solid conception of matter through the use of geometry. "So, extension in length,

PARTICLES AND WAVES

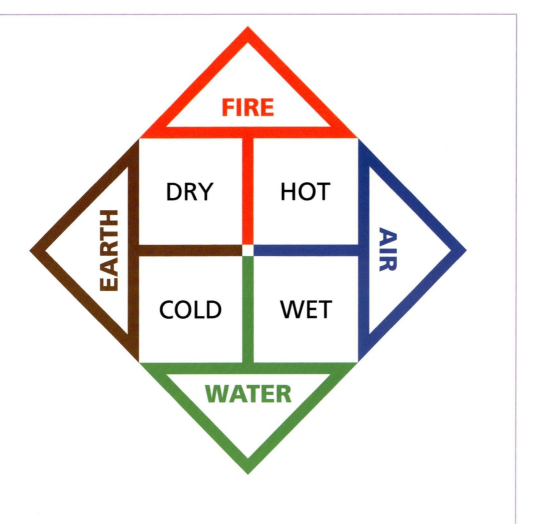

Empedocles's cosmic theory contained four elements, which were indestructible and unchangeable. But the forces he called love and strife could combine and separate the elements, creating the myriad of structures observed by the ancient Greeks in their everyday lives.

breadth, and depth, constitutes the nature of bodily substance . . ."[3] In other words, matter occupies a volume in space. Secondary qualities of matter, such as color and taste, are not inherent to matter but are produced by the perceptions of the observer.

Isaac Newton included the concept of inertia in the definition of matter. Newton conjectured that matter is made of "solid, massy, hard, impenetrable, movable particles."[4]

The standard model consists of fundamental particles, but they are not the solid, voluminous particles of Descartes and Newton. The particles of modern physics have no physical size and don't exist in any exact location. Newton saw the universe as a collection of billiard balls, moving through space and exerting forces on each other through gravity and collisions. Newton believed even light to be a particle, albeit one with zero mass that always travels at a speed of 299,792,458 meters per second.

Waves of Light

The idea that light is a particle was questioned by Christiaan Huygens (1629–1695) and Thomas Young (1773–1829). Young began noting the behavior of water waves in a ripple chamber in 1801. Waves differ from particles in many ways: both waves and particles propagate through space with a finite speed, but waves are spread out while particles are point-like. Waves are periodic, meaning they repeat after a certain amount of time, but particles are not. There are three quantities that specify the characteristics of a wave: the number of wave crests that pass a stationary point in a finite amount of time (frequency), the distance between two consecutive wave crests (wavelength), and the height of the wave from crest to trough (amplitude). Waves themselves are a subset of a more fundamental object called a field. A difference between

PARTICLES AND WAVES

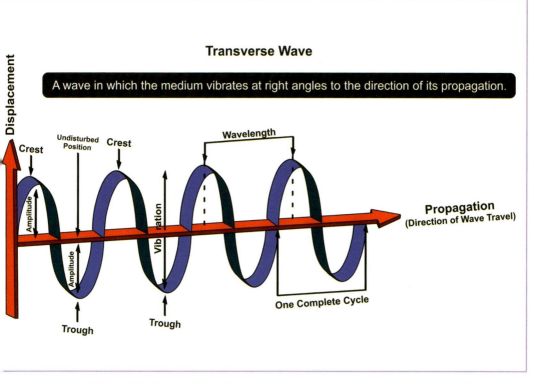

Waves can travel through a substance although the material doesn't move. For example, a speaker on one side of a room can transmit a sound wave to the other side by creating a disturbance in the air. The sound wave moves through the air while the air stays in the same place.

the classical notion of a field and the classical notion of a particle is that fields are continuous (i.e., fields exist everywhere while particles exist at just one point). Fields can be wavy, in which case they are waves, but they don't need to be. Imagine a box full of particles. The number of particles in the box could be huge, such as a billion or a trillion, but they could be counted in some finite amount of time. How could one similarly count the number of waves in a box? An equivalent question would be, "How many integers are greater than zero but less than ten?" The answer is nine. Now, "How many numbers are greater than zero but less than ten, including decimals or fractions?" There are an infinite number of rational numbers between zero and ten! There is no way one could ever count them all. These examples illustrate a characteristic of particles and fields, namely countability.

The ripple chamber used by Young was divided into two parts by a partition with two narrow slits, spaced close together. When a wave was created on one side of the ripple chamber, it would reflect off of the divider, except where the two holes were. The waves that passed through these holes continued into the other half of the ripple chamber and created an interference pattern. The interference pattern was a result of the waves combining; where the crest of a wave emanating from one slit met the crest of the a wave emanating from the other slit, the height of the wave doubled, and where the crest of one wave met the trough of the other wave, the height of the wave canceled out and was zero. At the opposite end of the ripple chamber from where the waves originated, Young could see standing waves, with points of constructive interference where the height of the wave varied rapidly, and points of destructive interference where the height of the wave never changed. The fact that waves combine by simply adding their amplitudes is known as the principle of superposition. There is no analogous principle of superposition for particles, so interference patterns are evidence of wavelike behavior.

A similar experiment of Young's used light rather than surface waves on water. A sheet of paper with a small pinhole in it was held up to the sun so that a collimated beam of light passed through onto two narrow slits of a second sheet of paper. If light behaved like a particle, Young would have observed a sharp

PARTICLES AND WAVES

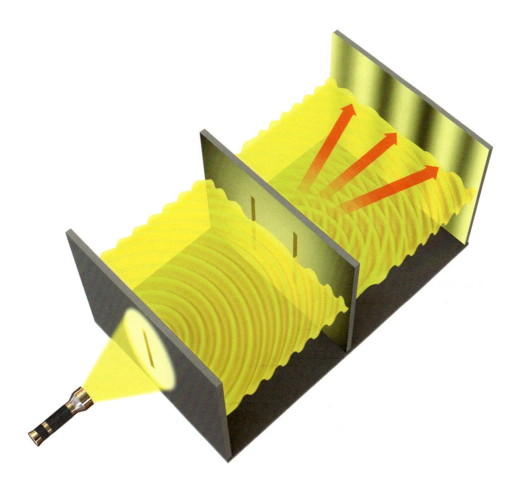

Thomas Young's double slit experiment showed that light recombined after passing through the two slits and interfered like a wave, creating a pattern of bright and dark lines, or fringes, on the viewing screen. If light behaved like a particle, only two bright lines would have appeared, essentially creating a shadow of the slit plate on the viewing screen.

image of the slits, like a flashlight shining on a person's hand leaves a shadow of their hand on the wall behind them. What he actually saw was an interference pattern, just like the one he saw in the ripple tank. Instead of only two bright slits he saw a multitude of bright and dark bands. The light was interfering with itself, just like a wave![5]

Sixty years after Thomas Young's double slit experiment, another physicist, James Clerk Maxwell (1831–1879), was reorganizing and adding to the theories of electricity and magnetism. A number of experiments had shown that a changing electric field created a magnetic field,[6] and a changing magnetic field created an electric field.[7] Maxwell combined these results to show that oscillating electric and magnetic fields would propagate through space as a wave. In 1864, Maxwell determined the speed of these electromagnetic waves, and, to his surprise, he found that they moved at 310,740,000 meters per second. This speed was so close to the speed of light that he concluded that light and electromagnetic waves were in fact the same phenomena.[8]

Particle Wave Duality

In 1900, German physicist Max Planck (1858–1947) was trying to determine the luminosity (amount of light being emitted) of objects at different temperatures.[9] Unfortunately, the math just wasn't working out. In order to get an answer that made sense, Planck had to assume that the energy of electromagnetic waves came in discrete clumps, or quanta. Planck considered this to be a neat mathematical trick, but to really understand the implications of what Planck had done took the genius of Albert Einstein.

PARTICLES AND WAVES

Electro-Magnetic Induction

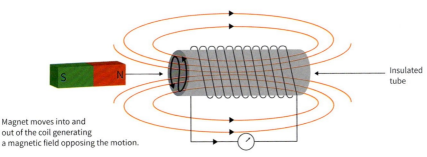

Magnet moves into and out of the coil generating a magnetic field opposing the motion.

An induced alternating current and voltage is generated.

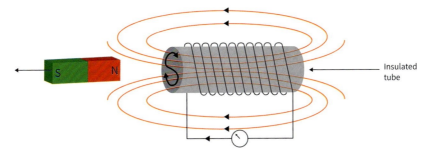

Oscillating Magnet Movement

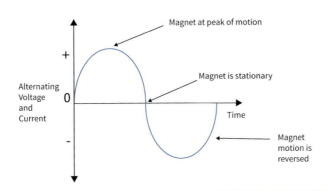

Moving a magnet into and out of a coil of wire sends a current through the wire because moving the magnet causes the magnetic field in the wire to change, creating an electric field in the wire.

33

THE HIGGS MECHANISM EXPLAINED

Einstein understood that Planck was counting light waves like one counts particles. Einstein called these particles of light photons. In 1905, Einstein used the photon interpretation of light to explain the photoelectric effect. When low frequency (low energy) light is shown on a piece of metal nothing really happens, no matter how bright the light is. But if the frequency of the light is increased above some minimum value (which depends upon the metal), charged particles suddenly start to shoot from the metal's surface, even if the light is very dim.[10] To make sense of this, consider a bowl full of green marbles. The green marbles in

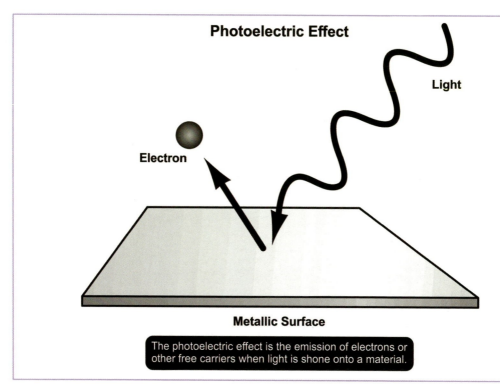

Photoelectric Effect

The photoelectric effect is the emission of electrons or other free carriers when light is shone onto a material.

For typical metals the minimum frequency required for the photoelectric effect corresponds to blue or ultraviolet light. For light below the minimum frequency, very few (if any) electrons will be emitted, no matter how bright the light is or for how long the light is shown on the metal's surface.

the bowl represent the charged particles in the metal; they are stuck inside the metal due to attractive forces in the atoms. Now gently drop in some red marbles, which will represent low energy photons. One will find that no matter how many red marbles one drops into the bowl, no green marbles ever come out. However, if one throws a red marble into the bowl with a large velocity (and thus a large energy), it will collide with a green marble and knock the green marble out of the bowl. One needs only one fast moving (high frequency) red marble to knock out a green marble, but even a million slow moving (low frequency) red marbles won't do anything at all.

EINSTEIN'S NOBEL PRIZE

The thing most people associate with Albert Einstein is the equation $E = mc^2$, which is a statement about special relativity. Einstein was awarded the 1921 Nobel Prize in Physics, but not for special relativity. It was his work on the photoelectric effect that ultimately earned him the distinction of Nobel Laureate. Another interesting fact is that the 1921 Nobel Prize in Physics wasn't awarded until 1922 because the Nobel Committee didn't think that any of that year's nominations satisfied the requirements outlined in the will of Alfred Nobel. The prize in that case was reserved until the next year, 1922.

The corpuscular nature of light led Einstein to conclude that light was made of particles, but Young and Maxwell had already shown that light behaved like a wave, so which is it? Is light a wave or a particle? This question led to the invention of a theory called quantum mechanics. Quantum mechanics treats matter like both a wave and a particle at the same time. This is known as particle-wave duality. Louis de Broglie (1892–1987) demonstrated in 1924 that electrons, very light and negatively charged particles that are part of what makes up atoms, are also wavelike.[11] If Young's double slit experiment is repeated by directing a beam of electrons instead of a beam of light at two narrowly spaced slits, an interference pattern will still emerge, but the separation between the bright and dark bands would be very small and therefore difficult to notice.

Early quantum mechanics used probabilities to describe the motion of massive particles, but only at speeds much slower than the speed of light. Paul Dirac (1902–1984) and others combined Einstein's theory of special relativity and quantum mechanics into quantum field theory to make predictions for massive particles moving close to the speed of light, but they soon ran into some very serious problems. In the same vein as Planck, the mathematics didn't seem to give sensible answers at high energies. Calculations in quantum field theory tended to give infinite results[12], which is a "canary in the coal mine" for physical theories, indicating that something is wrong. Quantum field theory was nearly abandoned as a reasonable theory of matter numerous times over the next few decades.

Then, once again, a revolution in physics occurred. Shin'inchiro Tomonaga (1906–1979), Julian Schwinger (1918–1994), Richard Feynman (1918–1988), and Freeman Dyson

(1923–) were able to find a way to fix the infinity problems in quantum field theory using a technique called renormalization. The end result was the quantum theory of the electron and the photon: quantum electrodynamics.[13] The success of quantum electrodynamics showed concretely that the fundamental constituents of matter behave like both a particle and a wave at the same time.

Chapter Four

The Standard Model

The standard model is a quantum field theory that describes three of the four known forces: the interactions that hold together protons and neutrons (the strong nuclear force), radioactive decay (the weak nuclear force), and electromagnetism. Evidence to validate the standard model primarily comes from high-energy scattering experiments, where particles are accelerated to extremely high velocities and then made to collide. By measuring how often different particles are emitted from the collisions, one can compare them to theoretical predictions and determine how accurate the theory is.

Predictions of the standard model are probabilistic, owing to the quantum mechanical nature of the theory. It is usually impossible to predict exactly what will happen in a single particle collision, but if an experiment is repeated a large number of times, the probability of a certain event can be predicted. For example, if two protons are collided, two photons with the same energy will be emitted—not every single time, but a certain percent of the time. The standard model predicts what this ratio should be so it can be compared with the experimental value to determine how well the theory agrees with observations.

A Property Called Spin

Elementary particles can be categorized by something called spin. The term "spin" is used because it is analogous to a rotating sphere, but particles don't have a physical size, so they can't literally be spinning. Imagine a basketball spinning about some axis: it can rotate around this axis with any rotational speed. This rotation gives the basketball angular momentum, which is conserved by Noether's theorem.

Elementary particles can also have angular momentum, but it only comes in discrete clumps given by the reduced Planck's constant $\hbar$ (pronounced "h bar"). The angular momentum of an elementary particle is called its spin, and it is very very small compared to the angular momentum of a rotating basketball. Fermions are particles that have half-odd-integer spin $(\frac{\hbar}{2}, \frac{3\hbar}{2}, \frac{5\hbar}{2}....)$, and bosons have integer spin $(\hbar, 2\hbar, 3\hbar,...)$. The difference between these types of spin may seem trivial at first, but it makes a huge difference in how particles behave. Fermions obey what is known as the Pauli exclusion principle: two fermions cannot be in the same location at the same time. Effectively, fermions feel a force that pushes them away from other fermions, so a large collection of fermions will tend to spread out and occupy a volume. This fits with the general intuition that matter takes up space. In contrast, bosons can pile up on top of each other, and an infinite number of bosons can occupy the same state.[1]

THE HIGGS MECHANISM EXPLAINED

Leptons

One group of fermions in the standard model are called leptons, from the Greek *leptós*, meaning "fine, small, thing."[2] Leptons are spin-$\frac{1}{2}$ fermions, meaning their angular momentum measured along any direction can be $\frac{\hbar}{2}$ or $-\frac{\hbar}{2}$. The leptons are subdivided into two categories: charged and neutral.

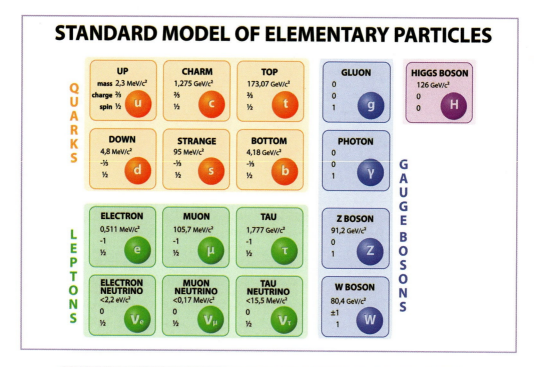

The standard model consists of quarks, leptons, gauge bosons, and the Higgs boson. The quarks combine to make up protons, neutrons, and particles called hadrons. Protons and neutrons then stick together to form the nucleus of atoms. Electrons, which belong to the leptons, are bound to the nucleus of atoms via the electromagnetic force transmitted by the photon, which is a gauge boson. The Higgs interacts with all of the particles except the photon and neutrinos and explains the origin of mass.

The charged leptons are the electron, the muon, and the tau. They all have the same charge and spin but different mass. The electron is the least massive of the charged leptons, the muon is moderately massive, and the tau is the most massive. There are also antiparticles associated with the charged leptons: the positron, the anti-muon, and the anti-tau. These antiparticles are exactly the same as their particle partners, but with the opposite sign of charge. The different charged leptons are called flavors.

The neutral leptons are called neutrinos, meaning "little neutral one." They were first theorized by Wolfgang Pauli (1900–1958) in 1930 to explain the loss of energy and momentum in nuclear beta decay, where a neutron decays into a proton and an electron. Observing the energy spectrum of the electron emitted during beta decay, Pauli noticed that it made more sense if a third particle was also being emitted. Because no one had observed a third particle in beta decay, it must be electrically neutral, and because the missing energy and momentum were small, it must be massless or nearly massless.

There are also three flavors of neutrino, one for each charged lepton. There is the electron neutrino, the muon neutrino, and the tau neutrino. Like the charged leptons, the neutrinos also come with antiparticles, but all neutrinos are electrically neutral. The masses of the neutrinos were originally believed to be zero, but observations of neutrinos changing flavor (oscillations) has shown that they must have some non zero mass. Neutrino oscillations mean that, for instance, an electron neutrino will turn into a muon neutrino and then back into an electron neutrino after enough time. However, the mass the neutrinos have must be very small, and in the standard model, all the neutrinos are considered massless. An extension of the standard model is required to give the neutrinos mass, which is discussed in chapter 6.

It is instructive now to summarize the organization of the leptons: there are three flavors of leptons: electron flavor, muon flavor, and tau flavor. Each flavor has one charged lepton and one neutral lepton. Every lepton also has an antilepton partner with the opposite charge but the same mass. In total there are (3 flavors) × (1 charged + 1 neutral) × (1 particle + 1 antiparticle) = 3 × 2 × 2 = 12 leptons.

The Photon

The charged leptons interact with each other via the electromagnetic field, introduced in chapter 3 as the photon, an electrically neutral, massless, spin-1 particle. The electromagnetic field is often written in terms of electromagnetic potentials, which contain all the same information as the fields but are often easier to work with mathematically. Physical theories written in terms of the electromagnetic potentials have a redundancy: an extra piece can be added on to the potentials without changing the forces acting on charged particles. In other words, there are multiple electromagnetic potentials that correspond to the same electromagnetic field. The ability to modify the potential without changing the physics is referred to as a gauge symmetry. Because of this, the potential is often called a gauge field, not to be confused with the electromagnetic field.

Charged particles interact with each other by exchanging photons. Imagine two ice skaters standing motionless ten meters apart on a frozen lake. If one skater throws a baseball to the other skater, the act of throwing the baseball will cause the first skater to accelerate backward. This occurs because of Newton's third law: in order to throw the baseball, the first skater must apply a force on the baseball, which causes it to accelerate forward. At the same time, the baseball applies a force equal in magnitude and in the opposite direction on the skater, causing the skater to accelerate backward. When the second skater catches the baseball, he will apply a force on the baseball to decelerate it. Once again, at the same time the baseball applies an equal and opposite force on the second skater, causing him to accelerate in the opposite direction of the first skater. After throwing the baseball back and forth a few times the skaters will be sliding away from each other. This is the same thing that happens when two electrons repel each other. The repulsive force between two electrons is caused by exchanging photons.

Quarks

Quarks are another group of spin $-\frac{1}{2}$ fermions in the standard model. Quarks interact via the strong force in addition to electromagnetism. The strong force is a lot like electromagnetism, but instead of having just one electric charge, there are three different charges for the quarks called color charge. Quarks come in either red, green, or blue, while antiquarks come in anti-red, anti-green, or anti-blue. Color is just a name for the charges and is not related to the wavelength of visible light. Quarks make up the proton and the neutron as well as other massive particles known as hadrons. Like the leptons, quarks are arranged into three different flavors, and each flavor has two quarks: the first flavor is the up quark and the down quark, the second flavor is the charm quark and the strange quark, and the third flavor is the top quark and the bottom quark. The up-type quarks (up-quark, charm-quark, and top-quark)

THE HIGGS MECHANISM EXPLAINED

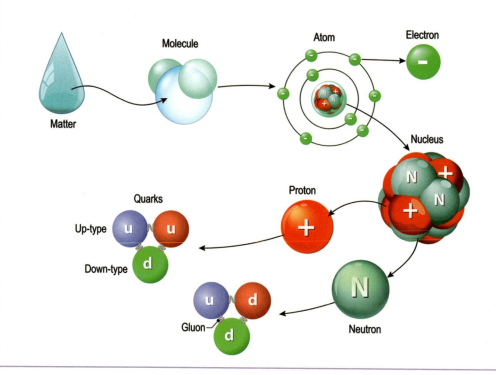

> Most of the mass in a drop of water comes from the protons and neutrons in the nucleus. However, the mass of the proton mostly comes from the strong nuclear force, the binding energy that holds the quarks together, and not from the mass of the quarks themselves.

always pair up with the down-type quarks (down-quark, strange-quark, and bottom-quark) like the charged leptons pair up with the neutrinos. The up-quark, charm-quark, and top-quark have $-\frac{2}{3}$ of the charge of an electron, while the down-quark, strange-quark, and bottom-quark have $+\frac{1}{3}$ the charge of an electron.

THE STANDARD MODEL

The strength of the strong nuclear force is, rather unsurprisingly, very strong. Quarks in hadrons are bound together so tightly that the amount of energy required to pull them apart is more than what is required to create new particles. Individual quarks are therefore never observed alone, but are confined within mesons (two quarks) or baryons (three quarks). The total number of quarks is (3 flavors) × (1 up-type + 1 down-type) × (3 colors) × (1 quark + 1 antiquark) = 3 × 2 × 3 × 2 = 36 quarks.

Gluons

The strong force also has a photon-like particle called the gluon. The gluon is a spin-1 boson that is exchanged between particles with color charge in the same way that the photon is exchanged between particles with electric charge. There are two major differences between the gluon and the photon: the first is that the gluon also has color charge. The photon is electrically neutral, so it doesn't interact with other photons, but because gluons have color charge they interact with other gluons. The second major difference is there are actually eight different gluons. The gluons are also gauge bosons like the photon, so in analogy with quantum electrodynamics (the theory of the electron and the photon), the theory of quarks and gluons is called quantum chromodynamics.

Weak Bosons

Every flavor of both the quarks and leptons has two particles. The electron flavor includes the electron and the electron neutrino. The first flavor of quark includes the up-quark and the down-quark. The reason each flavor comes in pairs is due

THE HIGGS MECHANISM EXPLAINED

to the third force described by the standard model: the weak nuclear force. The weak force is caused by three photon-like, spin-1 bosons called the weak bosons. The charges of the weak force are called weak isospin. Particles can have up-isospin or down-isospin, while antiparticles have anti-up-isospin, or anti-down-isospin. Using the leptons as an example, the neutrinos (e.g., muon neutrino) are the up-isospin particles while the charged leptons (e.g., muon) are the down-isospin particles. The up-quark, charm-quark, and top-quark have up-isospin, while the down-quark, strange-quark, and bottom-quark have down-isospin (the naming of some of the quarks might make a little bit more sense after learning their isospin). The weak bosons are usually written W^+, W^-, and Z^0, with the superscript indicating their electric charge. Besides being charged, the weak bosons differ from the photon in that they also have mass. In fact, their mass is the reason the force is weak. If the weak bosons were massless, like the photon, the weak nuclear force would be just as strong as the electromagnetic force. An example of a process controlled by the weak force is the decay of a down-quark (*d*) into an up-quark (*u*) by emission of a W^-, which then decays into an electron (*e*⁻) and an anti-electron neutrino ($\bar{V}_e$).

$$\underbrace{u + d + d}_{Neutron} \Rightarrow \underbrace{u + d + d + W^-}_{Proton} \Rightarrow \underbrace{u + u + d}_{Proton} + e^- + \bar{V}_e$$

This is beta decay of a neutron to a proton. The weak bosons are exchanged between particles with weak isospin like how photons are exchanged between particles with electric charge. Another subtlety of the weak force is that it violates something called parity.[3] Parity is a reflection symmetry, like a mirror. What this means is that the weak force looks different from its mirror reflection. Particles that feel the weak force are called

MARIE CURIE

The weak nuclear force is responsible for the radioactivity of some elements, where an atom of one type of element emits energy and changes into an atom of a different element. One of the major pioneers of the field of radioactivity was Polish scientist Marie Curie (born Maria Salomea Sklowdowska, 1867–1934). Curie coined the term "radioactivity" for the observed decay of isotopes of some atoms to a lower atomic number. For her work on nuclear decay, Curie was given the 1903 Nobel Prize in Physics, and she again won the Nobel Prize, this time in chemistry, in 1911. Marie Curie is the only person to have ever won two Nobel Prizes in two areas of science.

"left-handed," and it would seem intuitive to call the mirror image of a left-handed particle a right-handed particle. However, only left-handed particles interact via the weak force; right-handed particles do not feel the weak force at all.

The final particle of the standard model is the Higgs boson, discussed in the next chapter. Adding up all leptons (twelve), quarks (thirty-six), gauge bosons (one photon, three weak bosons, and eight gluons), and the Higgs (one), one finds that there are a total of sixty-one particles in the standard model.[4,5]

Chapter Five

The Higgs Mechanism

The Higgs boson is a massive spin-0 particle. It is a boson because of its spin, but it is not a gauge boson like the strong, weak, and electromagnetic bosons. The gauge bosons have an additional gauge symmetry that is really a redundancy in the theory. The Higgs boson is not associated with a gauge symmetry so that differentiates it from the other bosons. Interactions with the Higgs field give all the other particles mass. The basic idea is that the configuration of the Higgs field at low temperatures causes a symmetry to break, and all the particles that interact with the Higgs acquire mass when the symmetry is broken.[1]

Handedness

The standard model particles called fermions are forbidden from having mass by themselves. Fermions are composed of two parts: a right-handed part and a left-handed part. The helicity

HIGGS BOSON

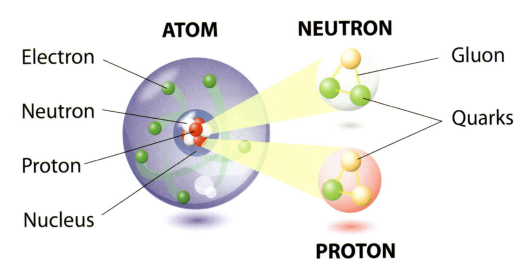

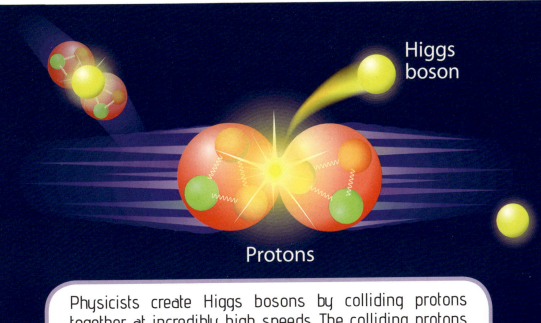

Physicists create Higgs bosons by colliding protons together at incredibly high speeds. The colliding protons explode into a vast number of different particles, and some of them are Higgs bosons. However, scientists never see the Higgs bosons directly because they decay very quickly. Instead, scientists observe the decay particles, usually two photons, using large detectors and trace them back to find that they came from a Higgs boson.

THE HIGGS MECHANISM EXPLAINED

of the fermion is the direction of its angular momentum (spin) compared to its direction of motion. Again, it is sometimes useful to think of spin as the rotation of an object, but remember that elementary particles don't physically spin. Imagine a basketball traveling toward you. If the basketball looks like it is rotating in the clockwise direction it is said to have left-handed helicity. If the basketball is rotating counterclockwise it is said to have right-handed helicity.[2] An easy way to tell if an object is left-handed or right-handed is to point your thumb in the direction of motion and curl your fingers into a fist. Then compare the rotation of the object to the direction in which your fingers curl. If the direction of the object's rotation matches the direction in which your fingers curl on your right hand then the object is right-handed. If the direction of the object's rotation matches the direction in which your fingers curl on your left hand then the object is left-handed.

A particle with mass can look right-handed to some observers but left-handed to other observers. Massless particles have the same handedness no matter who looks at the particle. Imagine two friends, Alice and Bob, try to determine the handedness of a spinning basketball. Alice stands motionless and observes the basketball traveling away from her to the north and rotating clockwise (i.e., the top of the basketball is rotating toward the east, while the bottom of the basketball is rotating toward the west). If Alice points the thumb on her right hand north, she will see that as she makes a fist, the fingers on her right hand rotate in the same direction as the basketball, therefore she concludes that the basketball is right-handed. Imagine Bob is in a car traveling in the same direction as the basketball. If Bob's velocity is greater than that of the basketball, it will look to Bob like the ball is traveling toward him. If Bob is also facing north, and the ball is getting closer to him, he would observe the ball

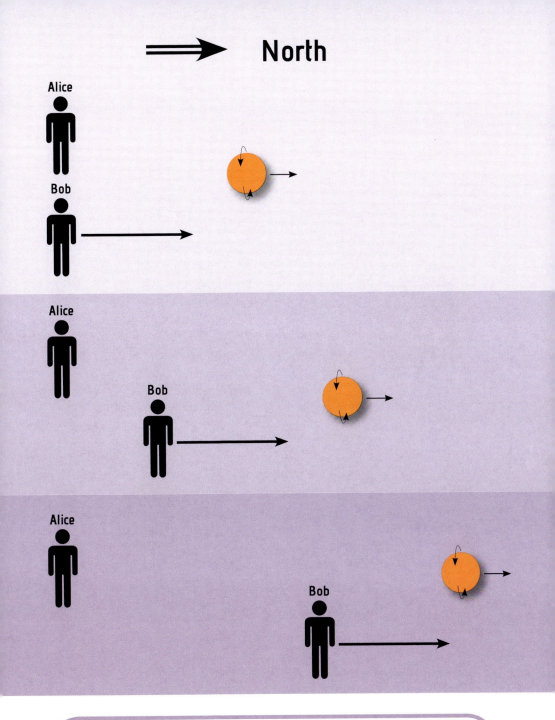

THE HIGGS MECHANISM EXPLAINED

traveling south. Alice and Bob still see the ball rotating in the same direction, but because the direction of the ball's motion has been reversed for Bob, he concludes that the basketball is left-handed!

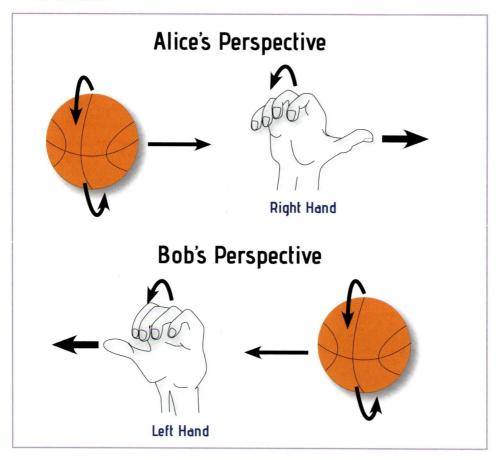

Both Alice and Bob see the ball rotating clockwise. Because the ball is traveling away from Alice, she points the thumb on her right hand away from her and observes that her fingers curl in the same direction as the ball's rotation. Bob sees the ball traveling toward him, so he points the thumb on his right hand toward himself, and observes that his fingers curl in the opposite direction as the ball's rotation. Therefore, Alice sees a right-handed ball while Bob sees a left-handed ball.

This creates a problem for massive fermions in the standard model because the weak nuclear force only interacts with left-handed fermions (and right-handed antifermions).[3] There is a contradiction because what one observer sees as a massive left-handed fermion interacting with the weak force, another observer could see as a massive right-handed fermion interacting with the weak force. No experiment has ever observed a right-handed fermion interacting with the weak nuclear force, so the only option that enables the theory to match observation is to conclude that the fermions of the standard model are massless. But the electron, the muon, and the tau have all been measured to have some mass, so how are these observations reconciled?

Symmetry Breaking

The way out is to have a Higgs field that interacts with the weak force and the electromagnetic force. The quarks and leptons also interact with the Higgs field. In the very early universe, the standard model has no masses and there is no problem with right-handed and left-handed fermions. But after a very short amount of time, about a millionth of a millionth of a second, the Higgs field undergoes a phase transition. Phase transitions are common in everyday experience. As water decreases in temperature, it transitions from a liquid phase to a solid phase at about 0°C (32°F) at sea level. The phase transition for the Higgs is similar to water freezing, but it happens at about one quadrillion degrees Celsius, or a thousand million million degrees Celsius.

The standard model actually has four Higgs fields. The gauge symmetry of the weak force means that the Higgs fields can be interchanged without affecting the predictions of the theory. This is like the earlier example of rotating a sphere about its center.

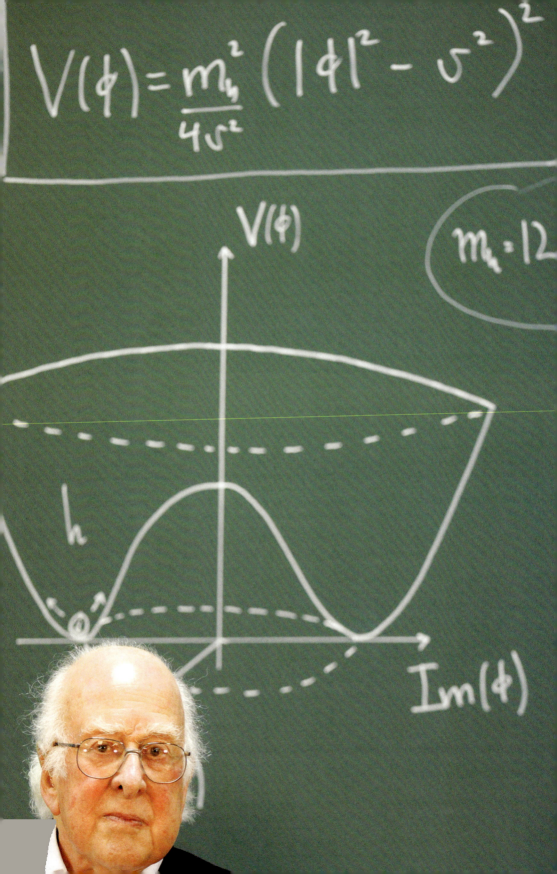

THE HIGGS MECHANISM

Spontaneous symmetry breaking occurs when the lowest energy state of the universe, called the ground state or the vacuum, doesn't respect a symmetry in the theory.[4] There is an energy associated with the Higgs field, often called the Higgs potential. The vacuum is at the bottom of the Higgs potential, where the energy is the lowest. Just after the big bang, the Higgs potential looks like a bowl, with one low spot in the center of the bowl.[5] If a marble is placed in this bowl, it will roll around until friction causes it to lose all of its kinetic energy, and it will come to rest in the center. Similarly, the vacuum is at the center of the Higgs potential because that is the lowest energy. The bowl and the Higgs potential are rotationally symmetric. If the bowl were rotated about its center, the marble would stay in the same spot. This rotational symmetry is a realization of the gauge symmetry of the Higgs field.

As the universe cools, the Higgs potential changes, and a ring forms in the potential that is lower than the center. This is often referred to as a "Mexican hat potential" because of its resemblance to a sombrero with an upturned brim.[6] A marble placed in a bowl with this shape will come to rest not in the center, but somewhere along the ring in the bottom of the bowl. If the bowl is rotated about its center, the marble will appear to be in a different location than it was before the bowl was rotated. The bowl itself is still rotationally symmetric, but the location

---

The Higgs mechanism is named after British theoretical physicist Dr. Peter Higgs. The Higgs potential after symmetry breaking looks like a bowl with a bump in the center (pictured behind Dr. Higgs). A marble placed in a bowl with this shape rolls down from the center to a point along the ring where the bowl is farthest down. This breaks the rotational symmetry of the bowl and results in the standard model particles attaining mass.

of the marble changes as the bowl is rotated around. One can imagine that the marble starts in the middle of the bowl before the ring is formed, preserving the rotational symmetry, then after the ring becomes lower than the center of the bowl the marble rolls down and spontaneously breaks the rotational symmetry. The Higgs mechanism works the same way: initially the vacuum is at the center of the Higgs potential, but it spontaneously breaks the symmetry once it becomes more energetically favorable to move the vacuum onto the ring.

The Higgs Boson

Physicists often talk about "the Higgs boson," not "one of the Higgs bosons." So why the singular reference if there are actually four Higgs bosons? After the vacuum spontaneously breaks the symmetry of the Higgs potential, a single Higgs boson acquires a mass and the other three remain massless and get "gobbled up" by the weak bosons. The three Higgs bosons that remain massless are referred to as Nambu-Goldstone bosons after Yoichiro Nambu (1921–2015) and Jeffrey Goldstone (1933–) who worked out the details of spontaneous symmetry breaking. When physicists discuss the Higgs boson they are talking about the Higgs boson that acquires mass after spontaneous symmetry breaking.

To visualize the Higgs mechanism, imagine looking down onto the surface of the ocean or a large lake. Waves on the water can move in any direction: north, south, east, or west. Imagine as well a vast number of buoys floating on the surface of the water. The buoys are evenly spaced, arranged in a square lattice pattern. As a wave travels through the buoys, they will move back and forth with the water. If a boat runs into one of the buoys, it will cause the buoy to oscillate, which will create

THE HIGGS MECHANISM

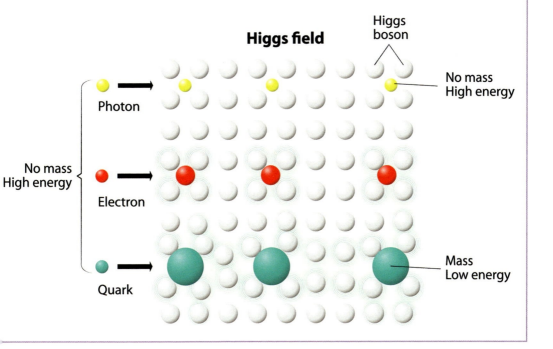

At very high energies, the particles of the standard model are massless. Even the particles that interact with the Higgs are massless at high enough energies. Once the energy decreases, the vacuum undergoes spontaneous symmetry breaking and the particles that interact with the Higgs field acquire mass. The photon however does not interact with the Higgs field, and so it never acquires a mass, even at very low energies.

waves on the water, which in turn causes other buoys around the crash to move. This scenario is much like the Higgs field in the early universe. The water is like some particle of the standard model and the buoys are like the Higgs field. The buoys interact by sending waves through the water, much like how particles interact by exchanging other particles.

THE HIGGS MECHANISM EXPLAINED

In the previous analogy, all the waves on the water move at the same speed, the counterpart to the speed of light in the standard model. The waves do not reflect off of the buoys as they move because the buoys move together with the waves. There is also a symmetry in this analogy: waves moving from north to south look just like waves moving from east to west if rotated ninety degrees to the left.

Now let the buoys undergo a phase transition. Attach the buoys to specialized anchors that allow only movement in the north-south direction. If you closed your eyes and spun around in several circles then opened your eyes again, you would instantly be able to tell which direction was north-south versus east-west because the buoys would only be moving in one direction. Being able to determine your orientation with respect to the cardinal directions in this way has broken the original symmetry of the system.

A consequence of this broken symmetry is that the waves will now reflect off the buoys if traveling in the east-west direction. Waves traveling purely in the north-south direction are unaffected by the anchors because the buoys still move with the water in that direction. However, when a wave traveling from the east toward the west collides with the buoys, some of the wave will pass through the space in between the buoys, while some of the wave will be reflected backward. The spaces in between the buoys will act like the slits in Young's double slit experiment discussed in chapter 3. The portion of the wave moving through one space interferes with the portion of the wave moving through another space. The interference of the wave with itself causes it to move more slowly through the buoys than it would have if the buoys weren't anchored down.

The broken symmetry reduces the speed of the waves through the buoys, but only in the east-west direction. The buoys had always interacted with the water waves, but it wasn't until the buoys were anchored down that water waves began to interfere with themselves. This self-interaction is the source of mass in the standard model, restricting massive particles to move slower than the speed of light. The Higgs field acquires a vacuum expectation value (often abbreviated v.e.v.), which is like the buoys acquiring anchors. The fields for the quarks, leptons, and weak bosons reflect off of the constant Higgs v.e.v., giving the particles mass.

THE HIGGS'S ORIGIN STORY

The Higgs mechanism was first theorized in a series of papers in 1964 by Robert Brout, François Englert, Peter Higgs, Gerald Guralnik, Carl Hagen, and Tom Kibble. In order to prove the theory, physicists would have to find the massive Higgs particle that the theory predicted. However, the technology required to search for the Higgs boson wasn't available for nearly fifty years. Despite the lack of experimental evidence, the standard model was developed in the 1970s assuming the existence of the Higgs, and the theory's ability to accurately predict observed phenomena was so astounding that many scientists were certain that it must be true.

THE HIGGS MECHANISM EXPLAINED

The Higgs Mass and Higgsdependence Day: July 4, 2012

The Large Hadron Collider (LHC) was constructed in Geneva, Switzerland, with the goal of finding the Higgs boson.[7] Two of the largest experiments at the LHC, A Toroidal LHC ApparatuS (ATLAS)[8] and the Compact Muon Solenoid (CMS)[9], measure the characteristics of particles created by colliding protons at nearly the speed of light. On July 4, 2012 (dubbed Higgsdependence Day), ATLAS and CMS announced they had found a particle that

The CMS at the LHC uses a 6-meter-diameter (19.6 feet) magnet to curve the trajectory of the charged particles. Charged particles move in circles in the magnetic field, and by measuring the curvature of their motion, scientists can identify the particle.

resembled the Higgs boson. The observed particle was a spin-0 boson with a mass between 125 GeV and 127 GeV (GeV, or giga-electron-volts, are units of energy or mass commonly used by particle physicists). Further research confirmed the discovery and determined the mass of the Higgs boson to be 125.09 GeV, or 2.23×10^{-25} kilograms (kg).[10]

In conclusion, in the early universe, when the temperature was very hot, none of the particles of the standard model had mass. Left-handed fermions and the Higgs interacted with massless weak bosons. Then the Higgs field underwent a phase transition, causing the vacuum to spontaneously break electroweak symmetry. After spontaneous symmetry breaking, the particles that interact with the Higgs field also interact with themselves, and the energy of their self-interactions is associated with their mass. The standard model still has electroweak symmetry, but the vacuum does not. The Higgs mechanism allows particles to have mass without breaking gauge symmetry or the left/right-handed couplings to the weak bosons. One of the Higgs bosons acquires a mass of 2.23×10^{-25} kg, while the remaining three Higgs particles get absorbed into the weak bosons.

Chapter Six

Beyond the Standard Model

As powerful as the Higgs mechanism is, it doesn't explain everything in the universe. The origin of the mass of the quarks, electron, muon, tau, and weak bosons was explained with the discovery of the Higgs boson, but three particles remained without mass: the neutrinos.

Neutrino Masses

When neutrinos are emitted from the sun, they oscillate between flavors (e.g., the electron neutrino turns into a muon neutrino). This could only be possible if the neutrinos have mass, albeit an extremely small one. Because neutrinos are electrically neutral, it is very hard to study them. The masses of the neutrinos themselves have yet to be measured, but the difference in masses between neutrino flavor has been measured. The Higgs mechanism gives no explanation for the origin of the neutrino masses, and it remains an ongoing investigation.[1]

Quantum Gravity

The standard model accurately predicts three forces between particles: the strong nuclear force, the weak nuclear force, and the electromagnetic force. However, the standard model makes no mention of the fourth force of nature: gravity.[2] A quantum theory of gravity has been quite elusive because it is hard to interpret physically. Another difficulty for quantum gravity is that gravity is so weak that standard model particles hardly feel gravity at all. To see how weak gravity really is, find a moderately heavy nearby object and lift it. The force you exerted on the object to lift it was greater than the feeble force created by an entire planet's worth of mass beneath you. The weakness of gravity makes it very difficult to probe at the small scales of particle physics because particles have so little mass that they hardly gravitate.

The Hierarchy Problem

Why is the weak force so much stronger than gravity? In order for the Higgs boson to be as light as it is, very large numbers must cancel almost exactly to get something very small, something particle physicists feel is unnatural. This is known as the hierarchy problem.[3] Many theories that extend the standard model aim to find a way to generate a light Higgs boson without this kind of fine-tuning. One such theory is supersymmetry. Supersymmetry introduces a new particle for every standard model particle but with different spin. Each additional particle cancels the quantum corrections to the Higgs mass of its standard model counterpart, thereby naturally leaving the Higgs very light. Supersymmetry is an elegant theory but has remained unverified by experiment.

THE HIGGS MECHANISM EXPLAINED

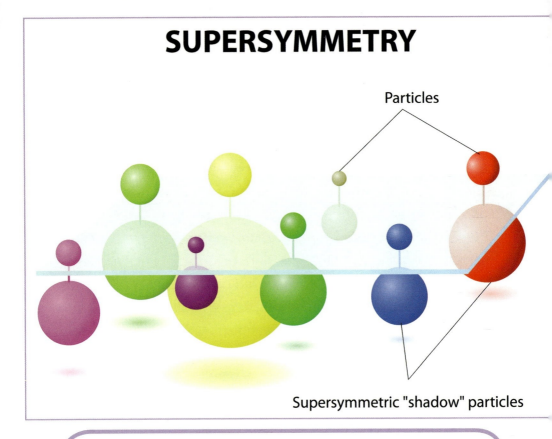

SUPERSYMMETRY

Supersymmetric "shadow" particles

Supersymmetry predicts that for every particle there is at least one super particle. For example, the super partner of the electron is the selectron, and the quarks have squarks. The photon super partner is the photino, and the super partner of the Higgs is the Higgsino.

Nineteen Unexplained Numbers

The Higgs mechanism explains that particles like the electron should have mass, but it doesn't predict what that mass is. To determine the mass of the electron, experimental physicists must directly measure it. Theoretical physicists then plug the electron mass back into their equations to make further predictions. There are nineteen such parameters (including the

BEYOND THE STANDARD MODEL

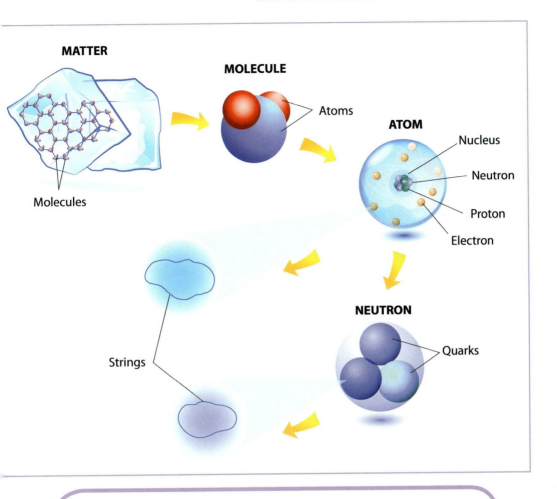

> String theory proposes that the fundamental particles of nature are not particles at all, but are actually small strings. The different types of particles observed come from the strings vibrating in different ways. The strings are so tiny that they look just like particles from far away.

electron mass) in the standard model that must be determined by experiment.[4] The minimal supersymmetric model, which is a version of supersymmetry, has even more unknown parameters—over one hundred! String theory attempts to resolve a great number of issues with the standard model, one of which is to reduce the nineteen unknown parameters

THE HIGGS MECHANISM EXPLAINED

into a single one. It is appealing to most physicists to think that there must be some underlying theory that predicts all of the parameters, but not all physicists believe this to be the case. The anthropic principle postulates that the parameters

COSMIC EXPANSION

Alexander Freedman (1888–1925) first theorized the concept of cosmic expansion in 1922 from using Einstein's theory of general relativity. Edwin Hubble (1889–1953) then measured the velocities of galaxies in 1929 and found that distant galaxies are traveling away from the Milky Way at a faster rate than closer galaxies. This discovery confirmed that the universe is expanding, giving further support for the big bang origin of the universe.

Freedman started the field of cosmology by using general relativity to predict the evolution of the universe. He found that Einstein's equations allowed for a universe that was expanding as time went on.

are random, that there is no theoretical origin for their values. If the parameters were any different than what we observe, the universe would not form structure and life couldn't have developed, so scientists wouldn't be around to measure them in the first place.

Dark Matter and Dark Energy

Dark matter[5] and dark energy[6] are also missing from the standard model and are unexplained by the Higgs mechanism. The rate of expansion of the universe, variations in the cosmic microwave background (radiation left over from the big bang), and the

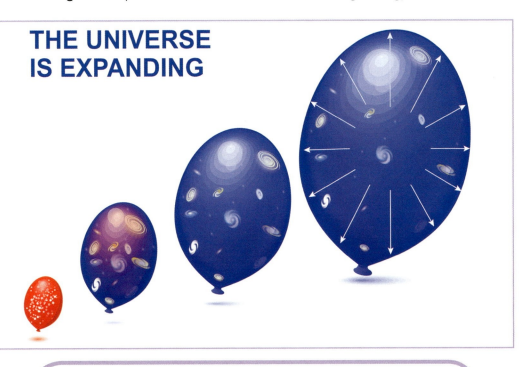

THE UNIVERSE IS EXPANDING

The universe is expanding like the surface of a balloon as it fills with air. Galaxies drawn on the balloon will recede away from each other, and the farther they are apart, the faster they accelerate away.

velocities of galaxies in clusters all suggests the existence of dark matter and dark energy, but what exactly those things are and how they behave is mostly a mystery.

The Higgs mechanism answers a question that has withstood explanation for millennia: what is the origin of mass? It is the interaction of particles with the Higgs field after spontaneous symmetry breaking, which creates energetic self-interactions. Great minds such as Aristotle, Isaac Newton, Albert Einstein, and others have pondered on this question and all have come up somewhat short of a satisfactory answer. The discovery of the 125 GeV Higgs boson was a triumph of human ingenuity and curiosity. Higgsdependence Day revealed the last missing puzzle piece of the standard model, yet physicists are left with more questions than answers. The great campaign to discover universal truth continues.

CHAPTER NOTES

Chapter 1
Making Sense of Mass

1. Wolfgang Rindler, *Relativity: Special, General, and Cosmological* (New York, NY: Oxford University Press, 2006), pp. 16–18.
2. Stillman Drake, *Galileo at Work* (Chicago, IL: University of Chicago Press, 1978), p. 20
3. Saintamh, "The Hammer and the Feather," YouTube, September 26, 2006, https://www.youtube.com/watch?v=4mTsrRZEMwA.
4. "Albert Einstein—Biographical," Nobel Foundation, from *Nobel Lectures, Physics 1901–1921,* Elsevier Publishing Company, Amsterdam, 1967, https://www.nobelprize.org/nobel_prizes/physics/laureates/1921/einstein-bio.html.

Chapter 2
Symmetries in Physics

1. Leon M. Lederman and Christopher T. Hill, *Symmetry and the Beautiful Universe* (Amherst, NY: Prometheus Books, 2004), p. 73.

Chapter 3
Particles and Waves

1. Stephen Toulmin and June Goodfield, *The Architecture of Matter* (Chicago, IL: University of Chicago Press, 1962), pp. 48–54.

2. Aristotle and William Charlton, "Books 1 & 2," *Aristotle's Physics* (Oxford, UK: Clarendon Press, 1970).
3. René Descartes, "The Principles of Human Knowledge," *Principles of Philosophy: Translated, with Explanatory Notes*, trans. Valentine Rodger Miller and R. P. Miller (Dordrecht, Netherlands: D. Reidel Publishing Company, 1982), p. 53.
4. Isaac Newton, "Book III, pt. 1, query 31," in *Opticks: Or, A Treatise of the Reflections, Refractions, Inflections, and Colours of Light* (London, UK: William Innys at the West-End of St. Paul's, 1730), p. 396.
5. Andrew Robinson, *The Last Man Who Knew Everything* (New York, NY: Pi Press, 2006), pp. 123–124.
6. Raymond A. Serway and John W. Jewett, *Principles of Physics: A Calculus-Based Text* (Boston, MA: Brooks/Cole, 2006), p. 809.
7. John D. Jackson, "Maxwell's Equations," *Science Video Glossary, Berkeley Lab,* June 5 2012, http://videoglossary.lbl.gov/#n45.
8. Joseph F. Keithley, *The Story of Electrical and Magnetic Measurements: From 500 B.C. to the 1940s* (New York, NY: IEEE Press, 1999), p. 115.
9. Helge Kragh, "Max Planck: The Reluctant Revolutionary," *Physics World* 13 (2000): pp. 31–36.
10. "The Nobel Prize in Physics 1921," *Nobel Media AB* 2014, November 11 2017, https://www.nobelprize.org/nobel_prizes/physics/laureates/1921/.
11. Richard Feynman, *QED the Strange Theory of Light and matter* (New York, NY: Penguin, 1990), p. 84.
12. Robert Oppenheimer, "Note on the Theory of the Interaction of Field and Matter," *Physical Review* 35, no. 5 (1930): pp. 461–477.

13. "The Nobel Prize in Physics 1965," *Nobel Media AB* 2014, November 11 2017, http://www.nobelprize.org/nobel_prizes/physics/laureates/1965/.

Chapter 4
The Standard Model

1. David J. Griffiths, *Introduction to Quantum Mechanics Second Edition* (London, UK: Pearson, 2005), p. 216.
2. "Lepton," Online Etymology Dictionary, November 11 2017, https://www.etymonline.com/word/lepton.
3. Bogdan Povh, Klaus Rith, Christoph Scholz, and Frank Zetsche, *Particles and Nuclei: An Introduction to the Physical Concepts* (New York, NY: Springer, 2006), p. 145.
4. Sylvie Braibant, Giorgeo Giacomelli, and Maurizio Spurio, *Particles and Fundamental Interactions: An Introduction to Particle Physics* (New York, NY: Springer, 2009), pp. 313–314.
5. Claudia Patrignani et al. (Particle Data Group), "Review of Particle Physics," *Chinese Physics C* 40, no. 100001 (2016).

Chapter 5
The Higgs Mechanism

1. Gregorio Bernardi, Marcela Carena, and Thomas Junk, "Higgs Bosons: Theory and Searches," *Physics Letters B* 667, no. 1 (2008): pp. 414–438.
2. Michael E. Peskin and Daniel V. Schroeder, *An Introduction to Quantum Field Theory* (New York, NY: Perseus Books Publishing, 1995), p. 47.

3. Chien-Shiung Wu, Ernest Ambler, Raymond W. Hayward, Dale D. Hoppes, and Ralph P. Hudson, "Experimental Test of Parity Conservation in Beta Decay," *Physical Review* 105, no. 4 (1957): pp. 1413–1415.
4. Vladimir A. Miransky, *Dynamical Symmetry Breaking in Quantum Field Theories* (Singapore: World Scientific Publishing, 1994), p. 15.
5. Philip Tanedo, "Why Do We Expect a Higgs Boson? Part I: Electroweak Symmetry Breaking," Quantum Diaries, November 29 2017, https://www.quantumdiaries.org/2011/11/21/why-do-we-expect-a-higgs-boson-part-i-electroweak-symmetry-breaking/.
6. Jeffrey Goldstone, "Field Theories with 'Superconductor' Solutions," *Il Nuovo Cimento* 19, no. 1 (1961): pp. 154–164.
7. "The Large Hadron Collider," CERN, November 11 2017, home.cern/topics/large-hadron-collider.
8. "ATLAS," CERN, November 11 2017, home.cern/about/experiments/atlas.
9. "CMS," CERN, November 11 2017, home.cern/about/experiments/cms.
10. Georges Aad, et. al. (ATLAS, CMS Collaborations), "Combined Measurement of the Higgs Boson Mass in pp Collisions at $\sqrt{s}$ = 7 and 8 TeV with the ATLAS and CMS Experiments," *Physical Review Letters* 114, no. 19 (2015): p. 191803.

Chapter 6
Beyond the Standard Model

1. Susanne Mertens, "Direct Neutrino Mass Experiments," *Journal of Physics: Conference Series* 718, no. 2 (2016): p. 022013.

CHAPTER NOTES

2. Anthony Zee, *Quantum Field Theory in a Nutshell Second Edition,* (Princeton, NJ: Princeton University Press, 2010), p. 172.
3. Matt Strassler, "The Hierarchy Problem—Of Particular Significance," Profmattstrassler.com, November 12, 2017, https://profmattstrassler.com/articles-and-posts/particle-physics-basics/the-hierarchy-problem/.
4. Robert N. Cahn, "The Eighteen Arbitrary Parameters of the Standard Model in Your Everyday Life," *Reviews of Modern Physics* 68, no. 3 (1996): pp. 951–959.
5. "Dark Matter," CERN, November 12, 2017, home.cern/about/physics/dark-matter.
6. Dennis Overbye, "Cosmos Controversy: The Universe Is Expanding, but How Fast?" *New York Times,* February 20, 2017, https://www.nytimes.com/2017/02/20/science/hubble-constant-universe-expanding-speed.html.

GLOSSARY

acceleration A change of motion or a rate of change of velocity.

active gravitational mass A property quantifying the strength of the gravitational field created by an object.

collimated Made perfectly parallel.

continuous Describes a quantity that varies smoothly and cannot be counted.

corpuscular Particle-like.

discrete Describes a quantity that is countable.

elementary particle A particle that cannot be composed of more fundamental particles.

field A set on which addition, subtraction, multiplication, and division are defined and behave as when they are applied to rational and real numbers.

gauge field A field that has a gauge symmetry.

gauge symmetry A redundancy in a physical theory that allows multiple fields to correspond to the same phenomena.

general relativity Albert Einstein's theory relating gravity to the curvature of space-time.

gluon The particle in the standard model responsible for the strong nuclear force.

hadron A particle composed of multiple quarks.

handedness The angular momentum of a particle or object along its direction of motion.

hierarchy problem The philosophical issue of the Higgs boson having a very light mass.

Higgs boson The fundamental massive particle of the Higgs field responsible for giving mass to the particles of the standard model.

GLOSSARY

Higgs field The field that describes the quantum mechanical behavior of the Higgs boson.

inertial mass A property of an object such that a force acting on the object produces a change in the object's motion proportional to its mass.

lepton A family of particles/fields in the standard model with half-odd-integer spin that participate in the weak nuclear force and electromagnetic force.

mass A property of an object generally quantifying the amount of matter composing the object.

passive gravitational mass A property quantifying the reaction of an object to being in the presence of a gravitational field.

phase transition The change of matter or a field from one state to another (i.e., liquid water to ice).

photon The quanta or particle of electromagnetic radiation.

principle of superposition A property of waves such that the result of combining multiple waves results in a single wave with an amplitude equal to the sum of the amplitudes of the constituent waves.

quantum chromodynamics The quantum field theory of the quark and gluon.

quantum electrodynamics The quantum field theory of the electron and photon.

quantum field theory The physical theory of quantum mechanical fields as representations of particles.

quantum mechanics The physical theory of probability waves as representations of particles.

quark A family of particles/fields in the standard model with half-odd-integer spin that participate in the strong nuclear force, the weak nuclear force, and the electromagnetic force.

THE HIGGS MECHANISM EXPLAINED

spin A quantum mechanical effect in which point particles have discrete values of angular momentum.

spontaneous symmetry breaking When the vacuum state does not respect a symmetry present in a theory.

standard model The quantum field theory that describes the strong force, weak force, and electromagnetism.

strong equivalence principle The equivalence of an object's active gravitational mass to its inertial mass.

weak boson The particle in the standard model responsible for the weak nuclear force.

weak equivalence principle The equivalence of an object's passive gravitational mass to its inertial mass.

weak isospin The charge of the weak nuclear force, in analogy to the electric charge.

FURTHER READING

Books

Bortz, Fred. *Understanding Higgs Bosons*. New York, NY: Cavendish Square Publishing, 2015.

Carroll, Sean. *The Big Picture: On the Origins of Life, Meaning, and the Universe Itself.* New York, NY: Dutton, 2016.

Carroll, Sean. *The Particle at the End of the Universe: How the Hunt for the Higgs Boson Leads Us to the Edge of a New World.* New York, NY: Dutton, 2013.

Hilton, Lisa. *The Theory of Relativity*. New York, NY: Cavendish Square Publishing, 2016.

Munroe, Randall. *What If? Serious Scientific Answers to Absurd Hypothetical Questions.* New York, NY: Houghton Mifflin Harcourt, 2014.

Pamplona, Alberto Hernandez. *A Visual Guide to Energy and Movement*. New York, NY: Rosen Young Adult, 2017.

Rovelli, Carlo. *Seven Brief Lessons on Physics.* New York, NY: Riverhead Books, 2016.

Websites

CERN

home.cern

Learn how the European Organization for Nuclear Research conducts experiments using instruments such as particle accelerators and detectors to study fundamental particles.

PhET Interactive Simulations

phet.colorado.edu/en/simulations/category/physics

Provides many visual simulations that help students get an intuitive understanding of physics phenomena.

The Physics Classroom

www.physicsclassroom.com

Free to use physics website with great tutorials developed primarily for beginning physics students.

INDEX

A
active gravitational mass, 10
antiparticles, 41, 46

C
conservation laws, 24–25
cosmic expansion, 66, 67
Curie, Marie, 47

D
dark energy, 67–68
dark matter, 67–68
de Broglie, Louis, 36
Descartes, Rene, 26–28
Dirac, Paul, 36

E
Einstein, Albert, 18, 32–34, 35, 36, 66, 68
electromagnetic force, 32, 38, 42, 43, 46, 48, 53, 63
electrons, 36, 37, 41–42, 44, 46, 62, 64

F
fermions, 39, 40, 43, 48–50, 53
force, 6
   types of, 38, 63

Freedman, Alexander, 66

G
Galileo Galilei, 10–11, 12
gauge boson, 40, 45, 47, 48
general relativity, 18–19, 66
gluons, 45, 46
gravity, 6, 10, 11, 17, 18–19, 28
   quantum theory of, 63

H
handedness, 47, 48–53
Higgs boson, 47, 48, 56, 59, 63
   discovery of, 60–61, 62, 68
Higgs field, 48, 53, 55, 59, 61, 68
Higgs mechanism, 9, 10, 25, 48, 56–57, 62, 64, 67, 68
   origin of theory, 59
Higgs potential, 55–56
Hubble, Edwin, 66
Huygens, Christiaan, 28

I
inertia, 12, 28
inertial mass, 10, 11, 12

L
Large Haldron Collider (LHC), 60
Leibniz, Gottfried Wilhelm, 12

79

leptons, 40–42, 43, 47, 53, 59

M

mass, 8, 10
   measuring, 9–10, 16
matter, defined, 26–28
Maxwell, James Clerk, 32, 36
muon, 41–42, 46, 62

N

neutrinos, 41, 46, 62
Newton, Isaac, 12, 28, 68
   laws of motion, 12–17, 42–43
Noether, Emmy, 23–24, 39

P

particle-wave duality, 36
passive gravitational mass, 10, 11
Pauli, Wolfgang, 41
Pauli exclusion principle, 39
photons, 34, 37, 38, 42–43, 45, 46
Planck, Max, 32–34, 36, 39

Q

quantum field theory, 36–37, 38
quantum mechanics, 23, 36, 38
quarks, 43–45, 46, 47, 53, 59, 62

S

Scott, David, 11–12
special relativity, 35, 36
special unitary transformation, 25
spin, 39, 40, 43, 45, 46, 48, 50, 61, 63
spontaneous symmetry breaking, 55, 56, 58–59, 61, 68
standard model, 8, 28, 38–41, 46, 47, 48, 53, 61, 63, 65, 67, 68
strong equivalence principle, 17–19
strong nuclear force, 38, 43, 63
superposition, principle of, 30
symmetries, 20–25, 46
supersymmetry, 63–65

T

tau, 41–42, 62

W

waves, 28, 29–34, 36
weak bosons, 45–47, 59, 61, 62
weak equivalence principle, 11–12
weak nuclear force, 38, 46, 47, 53, 63

Y

Young, Thomas, 28, 30–32, 36, 58